WALKING WITH ANGELS

Walking with
ANGELS

A HOST OF INSPIRATIONAL
AND UPLIFTING THOUGHTS

COMPILED BY

JULIE MITCHELL MARRA

THE C.R. GIBSON COMPANY

NORWALK, CONNECTICUT

Dedicated to my mom, my angel without wings.

Published by the C.R. Gibson Company, Norwalk, CT 06856 U.S.A.
Made in the U.S.A.
ISBN 08378-4999-3
GB796

CONTENTS

THE ORDER OF CREATURES IN WHOM THE HIGHEST
DEGREE OF CREATED PERFECTION IS REALIZED, IS THAT
OF THE PURE SPIRITS, USUALLY CALLED ANGELS.

St. Thomas Aquinas

INTRODUCTION

A short time ago, my entire life had changed. . . I got married, left my long-time job and moved across the country leaving all my family and friends behind. These were all firsts in my life. I left the security of the known to explore the unknown, and I was afraid.

During these frantic and intense times, my fear and loneliness made me very stressed and oftentimes sad. I wasn't really sure what made me upset or what helped me begin to feel happy and confident again. It was as if I had my very own guardian angel watching over my actions as well as my thoughts. Some divine intervention seemed to be happening in each area of my life. Whenever I felt completely out of control and ready to give up, one of the angels watching over me would give me a new breath and shine a new light in my life. Sometimes the outside factors of my life changed and sometimes the change was simply within my heart.

Life changes are expected in every person's lifetime. Throughout these changes in our jobs, families, friendships or lifestyle, it is important to remember our angels are always with us, guiding and protecting us.

When we are feeling discouraged and unhappy with ourselves or the world around us, an angel can somehow bring sunshine into our lives. It's a simple, but miraculous explanation for the hopefulness that suddenly appears.

Changes often bring fear. Being afraid is not something we care to admit but it is an emotion that needs to be reckoned with in some manner. We can only run from fear for a short period of time before it begins to eat away at our mental well-being. Fear will never go away until we face it head on. Looking at our fears as challenges to overcome will motivate us to conquer them. God's angels give us the unbelievably awesome power to overcome our fears and accomplish anything.

God sends his angels to us. They have the power to work miracles and to make our lives glow and radiate with happiness. When we have feelings of insecurity and we find deep inside ourselves the strength to conquer them, it is a Blessing from Above.

We are carefully watched and cared for by the Angels. Each time we look back on an event and think, what got us through that? The answer is simply, our angels. They may not be seen or heard, but they are felt in our hearts.

Who are the angels?

In Saint Thomas Aquinas' The Celestial Hierarchy, he explains the three different orders within each hierarchy of angels.

The First Hierarchy consists of those angels closest to God who contemplate the intelligible essence within God himself; goodness:

Seraphim
Cherubim
Thrones

The Second Hierarchy is made up of angels who preside over the ordering of the universe. They know the reason of things:

Dominions
Virtues
Powers

The Third Hierarchy of angels know the order of Divine Providence, and direct the ordering of human affairs:

Principalities
Archangels
Angels

Through the angels, as intelligences naturally full of intelligible essences, knowledge descends gradually from God, the source of all light, to man.

Angels lift us out of the traditional boundaries of time and into the ease of God's time.

When we experience a lost love, the death of a relative or the loss of security we must rely on our angels to show us a future bright and full of newfound hope.

Remember that we are watched and guided in life according to a divine plan. And our angels are there waiting to help us, when we open our hearts and minds.

Angels are present all around us, they are drawn to us by our emotions and actions. They steer us and guide us through losses and disasters. We are never completely alone.

Angels will always have our hearts in safekeeping. . . through many losses and new beginnings in life. Angels are truly miraculous gifts. Angels breathe fresh air into our lives, they play music to our souls and shine a beautiful light on our earthly existence with their divine presence. We give thanks for all the love and light Angels send our way.

In *Walking with Angels* you will hear from famous writers how angels affect our lives every day, emotionally and physically. It is my hope that the wonderful words of wisdom in *Walking With Angels* will help you as experience changes in your life.

–*Julie Mitchell Marra*

Realms of Glory During Times of Change

See, I am sending an angel ahead of you to guard you along the way and to bring you to a place I have prepared. Pay attention to him and listen to what he says.

Exodus 23:20-21, NIV

Make yourself familiar with the angels, and behold them frequently in spirit; for, without being seen, they are present within you.

St. Francis de Sales

Have patience with all things, but chiefly have patience with yourself. Do not lose courage in considering your own imperfections but instantly set about remedying them-every day begin to talk anew.

St. Francis de Sales

Angels are intelligent reflections of light, that original light which has no beginning. Wherever they are sent, they are there as mind and there can take on the power, but they cannot do this in more than one place at a time.

John of Damascus

Every visible thing in this world is put in the charge of an angel.

St. Augustine

"Angel" is the only word in the language which can never be worn out.

Victor Hugo

What know we of the blest above
But that they sing, and that they love?

William Wordswoth

It is not known precisely where angels dwell-whether in the air, the void, or the planets. It has been God's pleasure that we should be informed of their abode.

Voltaire

Have no anxiety about anything; but in everything by prayer and supplication with thanksgiving let your requests be made known to God.

Philippians 4:6, RSV

She hath no scorn of common things;
And, though she seem of other birth,
Round us her heart entwines and clings,
And patiently she folds her wings
To tread the humble paths of earth.

James Russell Lowell

Oh morning, at the brown brink eastward, springs-
Because the Holy host over the bent
World broods with warm breast and with ah! bright wings.

Gerard Manly Hopkins

The earth is to the sun what man is to the angels.

Victor Hugo

In this dim world of clouding cares,
We rarely know, till 'wildered eyes
See white wings lessening up the skies,
The angels with us unawares.

Gerald Massey

It came upon the midnight clear,
That glorious song of old,
From angels bending near the earth,
To touch their harps of gold:
"Peace on earth, good-will to men,
From heaven's all gracious King"
The world in solemn stillness lay
To hear the angels sing.
Still through the cloven skies they come,
With peaceful wings unfurled;
And still their heavenly music floats
O'er all the weary world:
Above its sad and lowly plains
They bend on hovering wing,
And ever o'er its Babel sounds
The blessed angels sing.

Edmund H. Sears

The guardian angels of life sometimes fly so high as to be beyond
our sight, but they are always looking down on us.

Jean Paul Richter

Silently one by one,
   in the infinite meadows of heaven
Blossomed the lovely stars, the forget-me-nots of the angels.

Henry Wadsworth Longfellow

Little eyelids cease your winking;
Little orbs, forget to beam;
Little soul, to slumber sinking,
Let angels rule your dream.

Eugene Field

He dreamed that there was a ladder set up on the earth, the top of it reaching to heaven; and the angels of God were ascending and descending on it.

Genesis 28:12, KJV

Sometimes on lonely mountain-meres
I find a magic bark;
I leap on board;
no helmsman steers;
I float till all is dark.
A gentle sound, an awful light!
Three angels bear the Holy Grail:
With folded feet, in stoles of white,
On sleeping wings they sail.
Ah, blessed vision! blood of God!
My spirit beats her mortal bars,
As down dark tides the glory slides,
And star-like mingles with the stars.

Alfred, Lord Tennyson

We trust in plumed procession
For such the angels go-
Rank after rank, with even feet-
And uniforms of snow.

Emily Dickinson

Angels we have heard on high
Singing sweetly through the night,
And the mountains in reply
Echoing their brave delight.

French Christmas Carol

Angels are bright still,
though the brightest fell.

William Shakespeare
Macbeth

The blessed damozel leaned out
From the gold bar of Heaven;
Her eyes were deeper than the depth
Of waters stilled at even;
She had three lilies in her hand,
And the stars in her hair were seven.

Dante Gabriel Rossetti

Angel voices, ever singing
Round Thy throne of light;
Angel harps, forever ringing,
Rest not day or night.

Francis Pott

Wing your flight o'er all the earth.
Ye, who sang creation's story,
Now proclaim Messiah's birth.
Come and worship!
Come and worship!
Worship Christ the new-born King!

Shepherd in the field abiding,
Watching o'er your flocks by night.
God with man is now residing,
Yonder shines the infant Light

Sages, leave your contemplations,
Brighter visions beam afar.
Seek the great Desire of nations;
Ye have seen his natal star.

James Montgomery

She is neither white or brown
But as the heavens fair,
There is none hath a form so divine
in the earth or the air.

Anonymous

Angels mean messengers and ministers. Their function is to exe-
cute the plan divine providence, even in earthly things.

Thomas Aquinas

None sing so wildly well
As the angel Israfel.
And the giddy stars (so legends tell)
Ceasing their hymns, attend the spell
Of his voice, all mute.

Edgar Allen Poe

Them heavenly born, or to be that same pair
Which through the sky draw Venus's silver team;
For sure they did not seem
To be begot of any earthly seed,
But rather angels or of angels' breed.

Edmund Spenser

Wings of Comfort During Times of Loss

And now it is an angel's song,
That makes the heavens be mute.

Samuel Taylor Coleridge

Golden harps are sounding,
Angel voices ring,
Pearly gates are opened,
Opened for a king.

Frances Havergal

Over all our tears God's rainbow bends,
To all our cries a pitying ear He lends;
Yea, to the feeble sounds of man's lament,
How often have His messengers been sent!

Caroline Norton

Tears, such as angels weep, burst forth: at last
Words interwove with sighs found out their way.

John Milton

Being a man, ne'er ask the gods for a life set free from grief, but
ask for courage that endureth long.

Menander

Sleep on in peace, await thy Maker's will,
Then rise unchanged, and be an Angel still.

Epitaph on the tomb of Mary Angell

There's quiet in that Angel's glance,
There's rest in his still countenance!
Angel of patience! sent to calm
Our feverish brows with cooling palm;
To lay the storms of hope and fear,
And reconcile life's smile and tear;
The throbs of wounded pride to still,
And make our own our Father's will!

John Greenleaf Whittier

And the wearied heart grows strong,
As an angel strengthened him,
Fainting in the garden dim
'Neath the world's vast woe and wrong.

Johann Rist

At that time men will see the Son of Man coming in clouds with
great power and glory. And he will send his angels and gather his
elect from the four winds, from the ends of the earth to the ends
of the heavens.

Mark 13:26-27, RSV

Angels descending, bringing from above,
Echoes of mercy, whispers of love.

Fanny Crosby

Go with me, like good angels, to my end;
And, as the long divorce of steel falls on me,
Make of your prayers one sweet sacrifice,
And lift my soul to heaven.

William Shakespeare

Love and Pity send their prayer,
And still thy white-winged angels hover dimly in our air!

John Greenleaf Whittier

But all God's angels come to us disguised:
Sorrow and sickness, poverty and death,
One after another lift their frowning masks,
And we behold the Seraph's face beneath,
Radiant with the glory and the calm
Of having looked upon the front of God.

James Russell Lowell

It is in rugged crises, in unweariable endurance, and in aims which put sympathy out of the question, that the angel is shown.

Ralph Waldo Emerson

Angel of Peace-thou hast wandered too long! Spread thy white
    wings to the sunshine of love!
Come while our voices are blending in song. Fly to our ark like
    the storm beaten dove!
Fly to our ark-on the wings of a dove! Speed o'er the far sound-
    ing billows of song!
Crowned with thine olive leaf garland of love, Angel of Peace-
    thou hast waited too long!

Matthias Keller

To comfort and to bless,
To find a balm for woe,
To tend the lone and fatherless,
Is angels' work below.

W. W. How

Soft as the voice of an angel,
Breathing a lesson unheard,
Hope with a gentle persuasion
Whispers her comforting word:
Wait till the darkness is over,
Wait till the tempest is done,
Hope for the sunshine tomorrow,
After the shower is gone.

Alice Hawthorne

Outside the open window
The morning is all awash with angels.

Richard Wilbur

Angels to Guide in Times of Fear

Mary was pledged to be married to Joseph, but before they came together, she was found to be with child through the Holy Spirit. Because Joseph her husband was a righteous man and did not want to expose her to public disgrace, he had in mind to divorce her quietly.

But after he had considered this, and angel of the Lord appeared to him in a dream and said, 'Joseph son of David, do not be afraid to take Mary home as your wife, because what is conceived in her is from the Holy Spirit."

Matthew 1:18-20, NIV

And God heard the voice of the boy; and the angel of God called to Hagar from heaven, and said to her, "What troubles you, Hagar? do not be afraid; for God has heard the voice of the boy where he is.

Genesis 21:17, NIV

These were the words that Virgil used to me,
And ne'er were tidings told that had in them
Such great capacity for bringing joy.
Within me more and more the longing grew
To be above: at every step thereafter,
I felt my pinions growing for the flight.
When all the stairs had passed beneath our feet,
And we were standing on the topmost step,
Virgilius fixed his eyes on me, and said:
"My son, you now have seen the temporal fire,
And that which is eternal; you have reached
A place where I myself can see no farther.
Thus far I have conducted you with skill;
Henceforth your own good sense must be your guide.
The step and narrow ways have all been passed.
Behold the sun, which shines upon your brow:
Behold the grass, the shrubs, and all the flowers
That grow so blithely in this region's soil.
Until you may behold those lovely eyes
Which, when they wept, brought me to succor you,
You may sit down, or walk up the meadow.

Expect no further speech or sign from me.
Your will, upright and sound, is now released:
You'll do no wrong, if you but do its bidding;
Wherefore I crown you sovereign of yourself."

Dante Alighieri

The best remedy for those who are afraid, lonely, or unhappy is to go outside, somewhere where they can be quite alone with the heavens, nature and God. Because only then does one feel that all is as it should be and that God wishes to see people happy amidst the simple beauty of nature.

Anne Frank

And the angel of the Lord called unto him out of heaven and said, Abraham, Abraham: and he said, Here am I.

Genesis 22:11, KJV

And Ganges' waters boil in heat of noon,
So stood the sun. The day drew to its close.
When lo, God's joyous angel shone before us. . .
Step forth, and make a trial for yourself,
With your own hands, upon your garment's hem.
In truth, all fear must now be put aside;
Turn here, and come in all security."

Dante Alighieri

Bond and Free
Love has earth to which she clings
With hills and circling arms about-
Wall within wall to shut fear out.
But Thought has need of no such things,
For Thought has a pair of dauntless wings.

Robert Frost

That is the fear she has—the fear
His soul may beat and be beating at her dull sense
Like blue Mary's angel, dovelike against a pane
Blinded to all but the gray, spiritless room
It looks in on, and must go on looking in on.

Sylvia Plath

The angel of the Lord encamps around those who fear and he delivers them.

Psalms 34:7, KJV

If you make the Most High your dwelling. . . then no harm will befall you, no disaster will come near your tent. For He will command His angels to guard you in all your ways; they will lift you up in their hands, so that you will not strike your foot against a stone.

Psalms 91:11-12, NIV

Angels and ministers of grace defend us!

> William Shakespeare
> *Hamlet*

I believe we are free, within limits, and yet there is an unseen hand, a guiding angel, that somehow, like a submerged propeller, drives us on.

> Rabindranath Tagore

Angel of the backward look
And folded wings of ashen gray
And voice of echoes far away.

> John Greenleaf Whittier

The angel said to them, "Do not be afraid; for see- I am bringing you good news of great joy for all people.

> Luke 2:10, RSV

Family Blessings From Above

It is very important to pray for others, because when you pray for someone, an angel goes and sits on the shoulder of that person.

The Virgin Mary
at Medjugore

Four angels to my bed.
Four angels round my head,
One to watch and one to pray,
And two to bear my soul away.

Thomas Ady

The Angel that presided o'er my birth
Said, "Little creature, formed of joy and mirth,
Go love without the help of any thing on earth."

William Blake

They are idols of hearts and of households;
They are angels of God in disguise;
The sunlight that sleeps in their tresses,
His glory still gleams in their eyes;
These truants from home and from Heaven,
They have made me more manly and mild;
And I know now how Jesus could liken
The kingdom of God to a child.

Charles Monroe Dickinson

In the old days there were angels who came and took men by the hand, and led them from the city of destruction. We see no white-winged angels now, But yet men are led from threatening destruction: a hand is put into theirs, which leads them forth gently toward a calm, bright land, so that they look no more backward; and the hand may be a little child's.

George Eliot

Abridge your hopes in proportion to the shortness of the span of human life, for while we converse, the hours, as if envious of our pleasure, fly away; enjoy therefore the present time, and trust not too much to what tomorrow may produce.

Horace

A baby is an angel whose wings decrease as his legs increase.

French Proverb

What though my winged hours of bliss have been,
Like angel visits, few and far between.

Thomas Campbell

My childhood's earliest thoughts are linked with thee;
The sight of thee calls back the robin's song,
Who from the dark old tree
Beside the door, sang clearly all day long,
And I, secure in childish piety,
Listened as if I heard an angel sing
With news from heaven, which he could bring
Fresh every day to my untainted ears
When birds and flowers and I were happy peers.

James Russell Lowell

As once the winged energy delight
carried you over childhood's dark abysses,
now beyond your own life build the great
arch of unimagined bridges.

Wonders happen if we can succeed
in passing through the hardest danger;
but only in a bright and purely granted
achievement can we realize the wonder.

To work with Things in the indescribable
relationship is not too hard for us;
the pattern grows more intricate and subtle,
and being swept along is not enough.

Take your practiced powers and stretch them out
until they span the chasm between two
contradictions. . . For the god
wants to know himself in you.

Rainer Maria Rilke

Little hands are clasped so tightly,
Roguish eyes with glances shy,
little feet go tripping lightly
Through the gates uplifted high.
Every little heart rejoices,
Clear as brooklets passing by;
Hear them sound their birdlike voices
Through the gates uplifted high.
Little feet keep tripping bravely,
Till their weary bodies die;
Then may angels guide them safely
To the portals of the sky.

                                    J. H. Kurzenknabe

You are the angel glow that lights a star,
The dearest things I know are what you are.

Oscar Hammerstein II

Long years have passed since that sweet time
When first I breathed upon the air
My simple little baby prayer,
A prayer with earnestness sublime;
Since first my mother clasped my hands
And bade me e'er I went to sleep,
Pray God my little soul to keep,
Take me to dwell in heav'nly lands.
And now the years on years have fled,
And tho' my head be bowed with grey,
The little prayer that I then said
Comes floating back on angel wing
As if, upon the other shore,
A little child had lisped it o'er
For God's own messengers to bring.

Eugene Field

Hush! my dear, lie still and slumber,
Holy angels guard thy bed!
Heavenly blessing without number
Gently falling on thy head.

Isaac Watts

A ministering angel shall my sister be.

William Shakespeare

May loving angels guard and keep thee, every pure as thou art now.

Anonymous

The angel replied, "I am Gabriel. I stand in the presence of God, and I have been sent to speak to you and to bring you this good news.

Luke 1:19, RSV

O little lambs! the month is cold,
The sky is very gray;
You shiver in the misty grass
And bleat at all the winds that
    pass;
Wait! when I'm big-some day-
I'll build a roof to every fold.
But now that I am small I'll pray
At mother's knee for you;
Perhaps the angels with their
    wings
Will come and warm you, little
    things.

Laurence Alma-Tadema

May loving angels guard and keep thee,
Ever pure as thou art now.

Anonymous

WHERE SHALL THE BABY'S DIMPLE BE?

Over the cradle a mother hung,
Softly crooning a slumber song;
And these were the simple word she sung
All the evening long:

"Cheek or chin, or knuckle or knee,
Where shall the baby's dimple de?
Where shall the angel's finger rest
When he comes down to the baby's nest?
Where shall the angel's touch remain
When he awakens my baby again?"

Still as she bent and sang so low,
A murmur into her music broke;
And she paused to hear, for she could but know
The baby's angel spoke.

"Cheek or chin, or knuckle or knee,
Where shall the baby's dimple be?
Where shall my finger fall and rest
When I come down to the baby's nest?

Where shall my finger's touch remain
When I awaken your babe again?"

Silent the mother sat, and dwelt
Long in the sweet delay of choice;
And then by her baby's side she knelt,
And sang with pleasant voice:

"Not on the limb, O angel dear!
For the charm with its youth will disappear;
Not on the cheek shall the dimple be,
For the harboring smile will face and flee;
But touch thou the chin with an impress deep,
And my baby the angel's seal shall keep."

Josiah G. Holland

Friendship Falls From Heaven

If we would cast the gift of a lovely thought into the heart of a friend, that would be giving as the angels give.

George MacDonald

Sweet souls around us watch us still,
Press nearer to our side;
Into our thoughts, into our prayers,
With gentle helpings glide.

Harriet Beecher Stowe

Rose-bloom feel on her hands, together pressed,
And on her silver cross soft amethyst,
And on her hair a glory, like a saint:
She seemed a splendid angel, newly dressed.

John Keats

Where the bright seraphim in burning row
Their loud uplifted angel trumpets blow.

John Milton

I, too, would seek the angels to follow
Lord of all Angels, wilt Thou me hallow?

Anonymous

It's food too fine for angels; yet come, take
And eat thy fill! It's Heaven's sugar cake.

Edward Taylor

Be not forgetful to entertain strangers: for thereby some have entertained angels unawares.

Hebrews 13:2, KJV

The golden moments in the stream of life rush past us, and we see nothing but sand; the angels come to visit us, and we only know them when they are gone.

George Eliot

Angels from friendship gather half their joy.

Edward Young

The angels' perspective comes from the vastness of infinity and beyond time; from there, they radiate love to everything without judgment.

Dorothy Maclean

Better than beauty and than youth
Are saints and angels, a glad company.

Dante Gabriel Rossetti

All God's angels come to us disguised. . .

James Russell Lowell

Once in an age, God sends to some of us a friend who loves in us. . . not the person that we are, but the angel we might be.

Harriet Beecher Stowe

The angels may have wider spheres of action and nobler forms of duty than ourselves, but truth and right to them and to us are one and the same thing.

E.H. Chapin

There are colors for every angel, color is something we see only in certain dimensions, but hues exist on the spiritual plane much finer than the colors we experience. When we let color speak to us in its true celestial language, we begin to communicate with angelic beings.

K. Martin-Kuri

Music is said to be the speech of angels.

Thomas Carlyle

In quibbles angel and archangel join,
And God the Father turns a school-divine.

Alexander Pope

Angels in the early morning
May be seen the dews among,
Stooping, plucking, smiling, flying:
Do the buds to them belong?

Angels when the sun is hottest
May be seen the sand among,
Stooping, plucking, sighing, flying;
Parched the flowers they bear along.

Emily Dickinson

It is not because angels are holier than men or devils that makes
them angels, but because they do not expect holiness from one
another, but from God alone.

William Blake

I want to be an angel,
And with the angels stand
A crown upon my forehead,
A harp within my hand.

Urania Locke Bailey

Nothing in this world is single; All things by a law divine in each other's being mingle.

Percy Bysshe Shelley

And while in life's late afternoon,
Where cool and long the shadows grow,
I walk to meet the night that soon
Shall shape and shadow overflow,
I cannot feel that thou art far,
Since near at need the angels are. . .

John Greenleaf Whittier

The Angels are spirits, but it is
not because they are spirits
that they are angels.

St. Augustine

I hide myself within my
   flower,
That wearing on your
   breast,
you, unsuspecting, wear
   me too—
And angels know the rest.

John Henry Newman

Every breath of air and ray of light and heat, every beautiful prospect, is, as it were, the skirts ofarments, the waving of the robes of those whose faces see God.

John Henry Newman

Make friends with angels, who though invisible are always with you.

St. Francis de Sales

Angels can fly because they take themselves lightly.

Scottish saying

Guiding Lights in Daily Work

Coincidence is God's way of performing a miracle anonymously.

Anonymous

Be of good courage, all is before you, and time passed in the difficult is never lost. . . . What is required of us is that we love the difficult and learn to deal with it. In the difficult are the friendly forces, the hands that work on us.

Rainer Maria Rilke

Hail, Guardian Angels of the House!
Come to our aid,
Share with us our work and play.
Be with us that we may hear your wings,
And feel your breath upon our cheek.

Geoffrey Hodson

Then an angel from heaven appeared to him and gave him strength.

Luke 22:43, Jerusalem Bible

Angel voices, ever singing
Round Thy throne of light;
Angel harps, forever ringing,
Rest not day nor night.

Francis Pott

But men must know that in this theater of man's life it is reserved only for God and angels to be lookers on.

Francis Bacon

This world has angels all too few, and heaven is overflowing.

Samuel Taylor Coleridge

Every man hath a good and a bad angel attending on him in particular all his life long.

Robert Burton

Though they are so great, so glorious, so pure, so wonderful, that the very sight of them (if we were allowed to see them) would strike us to the earth, as it did the prophet Daniel, holy and righteous as he was, yet they are our fellow servants and our fellow workers, and they carefully watch over and defend even the humblest of us.

Cardinal Newman

Oh, th' exceeding grace of highest God
That loves His creatures so,
And all his works with mercy doth embrace,
that blessed angels He sends to and fro.

Edmund Spenser

Life is so generous a giver, but we,
Judging its gifts by their covering,
Cast them away as ugly, or heavy, or hard.
Remove the covering, and you will find hidden beneath it
A living splendor, woven of love,
by wisdom, with power.
Welcome it, grasp it, and you touch the
Angel's hand that brings it to you.
Everything we call a trial, a sorrow,
or a duty,
Believe me, that Angel's hand is there.

Fra Giovanni

The Night of Glory, more opulent than a thousand moons!
then angels revelations waft down by the grace of the Lord.

Koran, XCVII

And yet, as angels in some brighter dreams
Call to the soul when man doth sleep,
So some strange thoughts transcend our wonted themes,
And into glory peep.

Henry Vaughan

If angels fight,
Weak men must fall,
for heaven still guards the night.

William Shakespeare
Richard II

We are all men,
In our own natures frail, and capable
Of our flesh; few are angels.

William Shakespeare
Henry VIII

May I burst into jubilant praise to assenting angels.

Rainer Maria Rilke

The feather, whence the pen
Was shaped that traces the lives of these good men,
Dropped from an angel's wing.

John Milton

My listening angel heard the prayer,
And, calmly smiling, said,
"If I but touch thy silvered hair,
Thy hasty wish hath sped.

Oliver Wendell Homes

An angel can illuminate the thought and mind of man by
strengthening the power of vision. . .

St. Thomas Aquinas

I throw my self down in my Chamber, and I call in and invite God, and His angels thither.

John Donne

Have courage for the great sorrows of life and patience for the small ones; and when you have laboriously accomplished your daily task, go to sleep in peace. God is awake.

Victor Hugo

God made us angels of energy, encased in solids - currents of life dazzling through a material bulb of flesh.

Paramahansa Yogananda

Everything we call a trial, a sorrow, or a duty;
Believe me, that Angel's hand is there.

Fra Giovanni

Angel of God, my Guardian dear,
whom God's love entrusts me here;
Ever this day be at my side,
To light and guard,
To rule and guide.

Traditional Prayer

Guardian Angels on Every Journey

After this I saw four angels standing at the four corners of the earth, holding back the four winds of the earth to prevent any wind from blowing on the land or on the sea or on any tree. Then I saw another angel coming up from the cast, having the seal of the living God. He called out in a loud voice to the four angels who had been given power to harm the land and the sea.

Revelations 7:3, NIV

And, behold there was a great earthquake: for the angel of the Lord descended from heaven, and came and rolled back the stone from the door, and sat upon it.

Matthew 28:2, KJV

God, which dwelleth in heaven, prosper your journey, and the angel of God keep you company.

The Apocrypha

My God hath sent his angel, and hath shut the lions' mouths, that they have not hurt me.

Daniel 6:22, KJV

And, behold, the angel that talked with me went forth, and another angel went out to meet him.

Zechariah 2:3, KJV

And there appeared unto him an angel of the Lord standing on the right side of the altar of incense.

Luke 1:11, KJV

Angels from the realms of glory,
Wing your flight o'er all the earth;

James Montgomery

For an angel went down at a certain season into the pool, and troubled the water: whosoever then first after the troubling of the water stepped in was made whole of whatever disease he had.

John 5:4, KJV

And they answered the Angel of the Lord that stood among the myrtle trees, and said, We have walked to and fro through the earth, and behold, all the earth sitteth still, and is at rest.

Zechariah 1:11, KJV

The angels are the dispensers and administrators of the Divine beneficence toward us; they regard our safety, undertake our defense, direct our ways, and exercise a constant solicitude that no evil befalls us.

John Calvin

And the Angel of the Lord came again the second time, and touched him, and said, Arise and eat; because the journey is too great for thee.

I Kings 19:7

For He shall give his angels charge over thee to keep thee in all thy ways.

Psalms 91:11, KJV

He said unto him, I am a prophet also as thou art; and an angel spake unto me by the word of the Lord, saying, Bring him back with thee into thine house, that he may eat bread and drink water.

I Kings 13:18

Hearest thou the strong wing
Of the Archangel, as it broadly sweeps
The empyrean, to the farthest orb,
Bearing Heaven's watch-word?

Lydia Huntley Sigourney

And when we cried unto the Lord, he heard our voice, and sent an angel, and hath brought us forth out of Egypt.

Numbers 20:16, KJV

I have spoken to thee: behold mine Angel shall go before thee.

Exodus 22:34, KJV

Angels, where ere we go,
Attend our steps whate'er betide.
With watchful care their charge attend
  and evil turn aside.

Charles Wesley

I will send an angel before you.

Exodus 33:2, NIV

And he said unto me, The Lord, before whom I walk, will send his angel with thee, and prosper thy way.

Genesis 24:40, KJV

God's Messengers
for all Who Believe

Are they not all ministering spirits, sent forth to minister for them who shall be heirs of Salvation?

Hebrews 1:14, KJV

There stood by me an angel of the God to whom I belong and whom I worship.

Acts 27:23, NRSV

Their garments are white, but with an unearthly whiteness. I cannot describe it, because is much softer to the eye. These bright Angels are enveloped in a light so different from ours that by comparison everything else seems dark. When you see a band of fifty, you are lost in amazement. They seem clothed with golden plates, constantly moving, like so many suns.

Pere Lamy

Praise the Lord, you His angels, you mighty ones who do His bidding, who obey His word. Praise the Lord, all His heavenly hosts, you His servants who do His will.

Psalms 103:20-21, NIV

It is a universal Catholic belief that not merely every just man, every child of grace, but in fact every single human being here upon earth, whether Christian or non-Christian, whether in grace or sin, remains during its entire life under the care of a Guardian Angel.

Joseph Husslein

An angel is a spiritual creature created by God without a body, for the service of Christendom and of the Church.

Martin Luther

A late contrition, but no bootless fear!
For when thy final need is dreariest,
Thou shalt not be denied, as I am here;
My voice to God and angels shall attest,
Because I know this man, let him be clear.

Elizabeth Barrett Browning

There is joy in the presence of angels of God over one sinner who repents.

Luke 15:10, KJV

And this is all that is known, and more than all—yet nothing to what the angels know—of life of a servant of God.

Newman

Praise ye him all his angels;
praise ye him, all his hosts.

Psalms 148:2, KJV

Millions of spiritual creatures walk the earth unseen, both when we wake and when we sleep.

John Milton

Hark! hark! with harps of gold, What anthem do they sing?
The radiant clouds are backwards rolled, And angels smite the
    string.
Glory to God; bright wings spread glistening and afar,
And on the hallowed rapture rings, From circling star to star.

Edwin Hubbell Chapin

Where were you when I laid the earth's foundation? Tell me, if you understand. Who made all of its dimensions? Surely you know! Who stretched a measuring line across it? On what were its footings set, or who laid its corner-stone-while the morning stars sang to all the angels shouted for joy?"

Job 38:4-7, NIV

Angels guard you when you walk with Me. What better way could you choose?

Frances Roberts

That's all an angel is, an idea of God.

Meister Eckhart

Now let us sing the Angels' song,
That rang so sweet and clear,
When heav'nly light and music fell
On earthly eye and ear.
To Him we sing, our Savior King,
Who always waits to hear.

19th Century Hymn

We shall find peace. We shall hear
angels, we shall see the sky
sparkling with diamonds.

Anton Chekhov

The seventh angel sound-
ed his trumpet, and there
were loud voices in heaven,
which said: "the kingdom
of the world has become
the kingdom of our Lord
and of His Christ, and He
will reign forever and ever."

Revelation 11:15, NIV

We should pray to the angels, for they are given to us as guardians.

St. Ambrose

Therefore for Spirits, I am so far from denying their existence that I could easily believe, not only whole Countries, but particular persons, have their Tutelary and Guardian Angels.

Thomas Browne

Angels are not etherealized human beings, evolving animal qualities in their wings; but they are celestial visitants, flying on spiritual, not material, pinions. Angels are pure thoughts from God, winged with Truth and Love, no matter what their individualism may be. Human conjecture confers upon angels its own forms of thought, marked

with superstitious outlines, making them creatures with suggestive feathers; but this is only fancy. It has behind it no more reality than has the sculptor's thought when he carves his "Statue of Liberty," which embodies his conception of an unseen quality or condition. . .

Angels are God's representatives. These upward-soaring

beings never lead towards self, sin or materiality, but guide to the divine principle of all good, whither every real individuality, image or likeness of God, gathers. By giving earnest heed to these spiritual guides they tarry with us, and we entertain "angels unawares."

Mary Baker Eddy

An Angel's Gift of Love

Fair ladies mask'd are roses in their bud;
Dismask'd, their damask sweet commixture shown,
Are angels veiling clouds, or roses blown.

William Shakespeare
Love's Labor Lost

Whatever pure thou in the body enjoy'st [said Raphael]. . . we
    enjoy
In eminence, and obstacle find none
Of membrane, joynt, or limb, exclusive barrs:
Easier than Air with Air if Spirits embrace,
Total they mix, Union of Pure with Pure
Desiring: nor restrain'd conveyance need
As Flesh to mix with Flesh, or Soul with Soul.

John Milton

Angels and archangels may have gathered there,
Cherubim and seraphim thronged the air;
But his mother only, in her maiden bliss,
Worshipped the beloved with a kiss.

Christina Rossetti

Whoever has not known
The arrows of your bow, O mighty Love,
Will never from above
Receive the light of faith from heaven's sun;
Nor know how lovers live and die as one,
Heedless of self, and living for each other;
How foolish fear and hope
Will with each other cope
Within the soul of a tormented lover;
Nor how the gods as well as men
    take fright
When they behold thy greatness
    and thy might.

Niccolo Machiavelli

The golden hours on angel wings
Flew o'er me and my dearie;
For dear to me as light and life
Was my sweet Highland Mary.

Robert Burns

Twice or thrice had I loved thee,
Before I knew thy face or name;
So in a voice, so in a shapeless flame
Angels affect us oft, and worshipped be;
Still when, to where thou wert, I came,
Some lovely glorious nothing I did see.
But since my soul, whose child love is,
Takes limbs of flesh, and else could nothing do,
More subtle than the parent is.

John Donne

Love is a power too strong to be overcome by anything but flight.

Cervantes

If I have freedom in my love,
And in my soul am free,
Angels alone that soar above
Enjoy such liberty.

Richard Lovelace

We are each of us angels with only one wing. And we can only fly embracing each other.

Luciano Crescenzo

The Book of Life begins with a man and a woman in a garden, it ends with Revelations.

Oscar Wilde

Look how the floor of heaven
Is thick inlaid with patterns of gold.
There's not the smallest orb which thou beholds't
But in his motion like an angels sings,
Still quirring to the young-ey'd cherubins.

William Shakespeare

God called the nearest angels who dwell with Him above:
The tenderest one was Pity, the dearest one was Love.

"Arise," he said,"my angels! a wail of woe and sin
Steals through the gates of heaven, and saddens all within.

My harps take up the mournful strain that from a lost world
    swells,
The smoke of torment clouds the light and blights the asphodels.

Fly downward to that under world, and on its souls of pain
Let Love drop smiles like sunshine, and Pity tears like rain!"

Two faces bowed before the Throne, veiled in their golden hair;
Four whit wings lessened swiftly down the dark abyss of air.

The way was strange, the flight was long; at last the angels came
Where swung the lost and nether world, red-wrapped in rayless
    flame.

There Pity, shuddering, wept; but Love, with faith too strong for
    fear,
Took heart from God's almightiness and smiled a smile of cheer.

And lo! that tear of Pity quenched the flame whereon it fell,
And, with the sunshine of that smile, hope entered into hell!
Two unveiled faces full of joy looked upward to the Throne,
Four white wings folded at the feet of Him who sat thereon!

And deeper than the sound of seas, more soft than falling flake,
Amidst the hush of wing and song the Voice Eternal spake:

"Welcome, my angels! ye have brought a holier joy to heaven;
Henceforth its sweetest song shall be the song of sin forgiven!"

John Greenleaf Whittier

To love for the sake of being loved is human,
but to love for the sake of loving is angelic.

Alphonse de Lamartine

I marked where lovely Venus and her court
With song and dance and merry laugh went by;
Weightless, their wingless feet seemed made to fly,
Bound from the ground and in mid air to sport.
Left far behind I heard the dolphins snort,
Tracking their goddess with a wistful eye,
Around whose head white dove rose, wheeling high
Or low, and cooed after their tender sort.
All this I saw in Spring. Thro' Summer heat
I saw the lovely Queen of Love no more.
But when flushed Autumn thro' the woodlands went
I spied sweet Venus walk amid the wheat:
Whom seeing, every harvester gave o'er
His toil, and laughed and hoped and was content.

Christina Rossetti

Twice or thrice Had I loved thee,
Before I knew thy face or name;
So in a voice, so in a shapeless flame,
Angels affect us oft, and worshipped be. . .

John Donne

Thou Fair-haired Angel of the Evening,
Now, whilst the sun rests on the mountains,
Light thy bright torch of love,
Thy radiant crown put on, and smile upon our evening bed!

William Blake

The Song that she sang was all written
In rubies that sparkled like wine,
Like the Morning Star burning, new litten
By the tablets of diamond divine.
Like some ravishing sound made from divers
Sweet instruments fluting in June,
From her soul; flowed those musical rivers of Rune.
Then come to my bower, sweet Angel!
Love's Fountain of Life to unseal.

Oliver Wendell Holmes

If I speak in the tongues of men and angels, but have not love, I am only a resounding gong or a clanging cymbal. If I have the gift of prophecy and can fathom all mysteries and all knowledge, and if I have faith that can move mountains, but have not love, I am nothing. If I give all I possess to the poor and surrender my body to flames, but have not love, I gain nothing.

I Corinthians 13:1-3, NIV

Good night, sweet prince: and flights of angels sing thee to thy rest.

William Shakespeare

The fate of the angels was definitely fixed from the first moment following on their creation; not as if they had been created in a state of bliss; but, once created, as is probable, in a state of grace, those among them who so willed, turned to God by a single act of love securing to them at once eternal happiness.

St. Thomas Aquinas

EPILOGUE

As my life is settling and some of the turmoil is over, I am beginning to feel more at home, more secure and more sure of all the changes I have made. After moving, I discovered how to keep in touch with old friends while making new friends. Being away from my family still hurts at times, but I guess that is what "going home for the holidays" is all about.

The most important thing I have learned is that every change in life is much more enjoyable if I release the stress, anxiety and worry and open my heart and mind to an exciting, undiscovered future. I have found peace and happiness knowing there are angels keeping my life on course.

May the prayers and promises of God's glorious messengers found in this book bring you hope and inspiration for many years to come. Keep this volume nearby during times of transition and whenever you need comfort in your life.

As you walk with the Angels, a change in your life will be a godsend and all of your goal's will be attainable, God gave us the

Angels to ensure that we find our destiny. Henceforth, may you find that your life will be guided by heavenly Angels through times of change, in your work and travel, family and friendships, and in faith and love.

—*Julie Mitchell Marra*

ACKNOWLEDGEMENTS

The editor and the publisher have made every effort to trace the ownership of all copyrighted material and to secure permission from copyright holders of such material. In the event of any question arising as to the use of any material, the publisher and editor, while expressing regret for inadvertent error, will be pleased to make the necessary corrections in future printings. Thanks are due to the following authors, publishers, publications and agents for permission to use the material indicated.

Scripture verses marked (TLB) are taken from *The Living Bible*, copyright 1971. Used by permission of Tyndale House Publishers, Inc., Wheaton, IL 60189. All rights reserved.

Scripture verses marked RSV are taken from the *Revised Standard Version of the Bible*, copyright 1946, 1952, 1971, 1973, Division of Christian Education, National Council of the Churches of Christ in the USA. All rights reserved.

$\mathscr{A}$CKNOWLEDGEMENTS

Scripture verses marked NIV are taken from the *Holy Bible, New International Version*®. NIV® Copyright 1973, 1978, 1984 by International Bible Society. Used by permission of Zondervan Publishing House. All rights reserved.

Scripture marked KJV is from the *King James Version* of the Bible.

Harper Collins, Excerpt from *The Poems of Sylvia Plath* © Sylvia Plath. Published by Harper Collins, New York, NY.

Theosophical Publishing House, Excerpt by Geoffrey Hodson used with permission of Theosophical Publishing House, Wheaton, IL.

Little Brown & Company, Excerpts from *The Collected Poems of Emily Dickinson* © 1982 Little Brown & Co.

Harcourt Brace & Company, Excerpt from *Love Calls Us to the Things of This World* © 1956, 1984 Richard Wilbur. Permission granted by Harcourt Brace & Company.

Polygram International, Excerpt from *All The Things You Are* by Oscar Hammerstein © Polygram International, Los Angeles, CA.

Editor: Eileen Mulkerin D'Andrea

Book design: Susan Hood

Type set in Centaur